ON THE
DOORSTEP

On the Doorstep

POEMS BY
Susan Shaw Sailer

Shanti Arts Publishing

Brunswick, Maine

ON THE DOORSTEP

Published by Shanti Arts Publishing

Designed by Shanti Arts Designs

Cover image by Tom Miles and used with his permission.

Shanti Arts LLC
193 Hillside Road
Brunswick, Maine 04011
shantiarts.com

Printed in the United States of America

ISBN: 978-1-962082-70-9 (softcover)

Library of Congress Control Number (LCCN): 2025937120

To Earth's children,
All of them

Contents

Acknowledgements   9

I.

Mutual Attraction . . .   12
Years Amble through Me . . .   13
Plans for a Productive Day . . .   14
The Cost . . .   15
New Sight . . .   16
Brightness Calls . . .   17
Spotlight . . .   18
on the doorstep . . .   19
Home . . .   20
Squid Jigging . . .   21
Ghost Music for Shipwrecks . . .   22
Hallelujah . . .   23

II.

Suppose . . .   26
Sisyphus on Strings . . .   28
Yesterday's Takeout . . .   29
Incidents for the Forgettery . . .   30
Riding the Womb of the Last Wave . . .   32
I saw a leatherback sea turtle . . .   33
Q & A Session . . .   34
Were They Real? Where Did They Go? . . .   35
Texas Hold'em . . .   36
Make It Red . . .   37
Death Grabs the Pommel Mounts,
    Rides Off . . .   38
Still   39
Ode to This Body Coming Up
    on Eighty-Four Years . . .   40
Cache . . .   41
chaos descended . . .   42

III.

Grief Speaks . . .   46

Learning to Hum . . .   48

At Five I Learn Delight . . .   49

Ode to My Hearing Aids on Valentine's Day . . .   50

Hope Is a Gizzard, . . .   51

The Asteroid . . .   52

Out of Hopeful Green Stuff . . .   53

Hairstory . . .   54

Unraveling . . .   56

My First, My Last . . .   57

Tossing the Dice of Language . . .   58

IV.

Your Name Is a Wound Is a Song . . .   62

Sometimes I Disappear . . .   64

Spring . . .   65

To Be or Not To Be . . .   66

Hidden Valley Liturgy . . .   67

Heart . . .   68

Hope Is a Grasshopper . . .   69

Silent before Eternity . . .   70

My Life with Rivers . . .   71

The Suitor . . .   72

Twenty Existential Questions . . .   74

Time, . . .   76

Notes . . .   79

Acknowledgements

I thank the editors and staff of the following publications where these poems first appeared, sometimes in earlier versions and titles:

Atlanta Review: "Squid Jigging"

from the ends of the earth: poems of the Eco-Justice for All! Inquiry, eds. Celeste Gainey and Erin Roussel: "The Asteroid"

Gyroscope Review: "Twenty Existential Questions"

One Art: "My Life with Rivers"; "Texas Hold-Em"; and "Your Name Is a Wound Is a Song"

Persimmon Tree: "Hidden Valley Liturgy"

Slipstream: "Sisyphus on Strings"

Thanks to my beloved partner, Tom Miles, always first reader of these poems.

Thanks also to Nancy Krygowski and members of her Madwomen online classes, to Pauletta Hansel and members of her Draft to Craft classes, and to Richard Hague and Sherry Cook Stanforth's Writers Table and its members. All of these people helped my poems grow.

I'm grateful to Rebecca Cole-Turner, Kay Comini, Liane Norman, M. A. Sinnhuber, Jamie Benjamin, and Marilyn Noll for their suggestions.

Gratitude to my online writing partners Lynne McMahon, Janet Barry, Roberta Feins, and John Krumberger.

Special thanks to April Ossmann, whose suggestions transformed this manuscript, helped me re-vision it, helped it grow up.

I.

the cool nights you thought
of home and that voicelessness
wears round too
that was present in its vining
the slow way you found
nothing to hold, or did and
pulled farther into the findings.

——Ed Skoog

Mutual Attraction

A tawny length stretches high above me
on a dead oak branch, Sonoran Desert Zoo,
the 25-foot fence my security against
his strength, though only his tail's
twitching black tip suggests intent.

His yellow eyes don't leave mine,
neither predator eyeing prey nor
possible companion. Do I hold
his interest over the squirrel below me
only for my superior size?
Or for my caging kind?

I don't go on to see the desert hare—
some bond holds between the mountain lion
and me, that relaxed power elongated on a limb.

I wonder how it feels to wear his muscles.
I sense them fueling thighs and back,
as in a dream where I am me, and also me
observing me. Do I want that power?
No. It terrifies the little child in me,
old woman that I am.

Years Amble through Me

As I play Ravel's *Valses Noble Et Sentimentales*
on the piano, summer beckons through glass,
a few sun-struck strawberries glisten as another
summer floods me: relaxing at the mountain home
my parents built for their retirement. Ten, my daughter
sits on the wrap-around deck examining a beetle
she palmed on a morning forest walk. Dad's still
strong enough to run the chain saw, down old firs
that winds could fell, crush the cabin's roof.
Mother brings iced tea. We sit and sip coolness,
enjoy August heat. Memory leaves me breathless,
fingers sit unmoving on the keys, both parents gone,
my child the mother of adults.

Plans for a Productive Day

Though shimmer's magic allows for loss and gloss,
        don't get lost in glitter.
Every moving train is leaving somewhere
        opening portals to tomorrow that close behind them.
I see a patch of what looks like light. Closer, I find it's reflection,
        photons scattered, bouncing off a mirror.
I'm drifting,
        so why not take reflected light for meaning I want to
        make?
Better at chaos than chess, I know the gate ahead
        doesn't mean the end.
I pivot when the line turns, like its hinges, power straight ahead,
        take remnants of light for the thing itself.
Who can know what's real when quantum physics says
        perception affects reality? The gate's here now.
Shall I turn back, sit and wait, or take the next train
        out of town?
Choose quotidian or mystery?

The Cost

Already in our seventies, we sold our cottage
on the steep hill fronting Rock Lake formed
fifty years ago by damming Glady Creek,
small cabins encircling it. We didn't sell

for lack of space, we didn't need much at
our age. We sold to escape winter roads,
their mean curves, ice and snow's silent
koans of would-we make-it-safely-home.

Once moved into a town condo, we didn't
miss Canada geese pooping everywhere,
deer eating plants supposed to be deer-proof,
my car slipping on ice, nearly hitting a tree

off our steep driveway, wind-driven snow
blocking the door, locking us in, spring
rains flooding the road so we couldn't drive
home. What we missed were does and fawns

grazing on the lawn, black bears climbing
bird feeder poles for seeds, coyotes singing
in the hills a bedtime lullaby. Chose safety
over beloved place. The cost, a slow soul burn.

New Sight

That I see rain dripping from the roof
from last night's storm is blessing.
I know despite my eyes' disease

(*You'll probably never be completely
blind*, my doctor said) my ease in seeing
a maple leaf's five lobes, its autumn gold

speckled with black mold, keeps me in touch
with earth's wonder, though already I can't tell
dark green from navy blue or black. I trust

that as my vision dims (already I confuse *m*
and *n*) other wonders will comfort and sustain,
leading me from my condo to where Glady Creek

joins Rock Lake, runs to Tygart River, which flows
into the Monongahela, which gives up its identity
to join the Ohio. All this shows how parts form

greater wholes, how I'm a small gold leaf carried
by last night's rain toward a stream I don't see but
sense. It pillows my fading weight as I rush between

rain-darkened stream banks toward some greater joining.

Brightness Calls

This morning-glory-blue sky
shines so deep I could step into it
and go on to my beyond. In long silence
a dove plays hide and seek with raptor
consequences. I tell my heart, *stop*
playing with the brightness between
words and take communion—go
over there and kiss him.

This morning-glory sky stakes
blue so deep I could leap into it
and live a dream. After silence
a dove plays hide and seek,
so when I ask my heart to hear
the difference between how words
sound and what they mean,
brightness answers with a dance.

This morning sky offers morning-
glory-blue tinged with pink.
I could hang-glide, but winds
blow unpredictable. I tire of reticence,
of not saying how each person's
brightness kisses me with difference
that grows and grounds me,
each one beauteous.

Spotlight

—for Jan Beatty

This morning when I woke, four fingers refused
to loosen, throw off bed covers. It's just arthritis,
could be worse. If I wait, they'll unbend. The trick
is patience—of which you and I have so little.
My left hip's okay with the condo's tiny distances,
but show it a stream, let it hear water ripple over stones,
that hip takes 12 steps and stops. Says walks hurt.

Well, there's hurt and there's *hurt*. The latter's the kind
I'm dealing with. If tomorrow's MRI declares these bones
should go, I'll keep the new titanium set, inscribe with
thanks for your *Write the body* the originals to you,
These old bones that once loved walking now rest in peace—
in the curio cabinet I'm assembling, one I spotlight every
night to highlight how eloquently this old body will go.

on the doorstep

something I can't quite hear piques my ears
a bee buzzes inside a jar
swallows scissor the sky
bottled messages hide at sea
(who frees the bee
finds the messages
collects the scissorings)

tempus fugit
the mystery of to be
or not to be
always just ahead of me
in some fog
I try to comprehend the question
is that You

birds trill aubades
sun greets summer earth
wind whiffles tree tops
as the pandemic razes bodies
fires burn forests, towns
crime rages in cities
hate rampages
where does hope hide
where are You
my daughter calls from Peru to say she's fine
my lover tells a corny joke that makes me laugh
are You there too   love's origin and guarantor
this emptiness I feel that seeks to fill itself

You, invisible

Home

The objects I've collected speak to me
from condo walls—Navajo rugs whose

balanced horizontals and verticals proclaim
a stable order, an Inuit woman transforming

to a deer, inside a human head an owl, a fish,
a beaver, water joining water photos—a West

Virginia crashing waterfall, Pacific Ocean
bursting through a blow hole off the Oregon coast.

Others speak from tables—Navajo and
Acoma pots, blue polished glass shot hot

from an Indonesian volcano, Pacific half
clam shell, Atlantic snail-devoured conch.

Still others watch from shelves—African
masks of trickster, warrior, healer; American

Indigenous soapstone carvings, Maine granite
hunk, small stones I picked up. Riverbeds

and trails my home in the world, the world
in my home.

Squid Jigging

Say those words out loud—squishy, soft,
two accents, like two eyes a boat's lights.
Get the scene: a boat's lights shine at night
on sea, where squids rise, soft, squishy, light-
drawn, skin camouflaging as they surface,
pulsing dots of color, from dark to sparkling.
Jig lures tempt them to latch on, pulled up
to become starters for your next meal.
Sometimes, what lies deep shouldn't surface
when bright lights lure. Hold to the dark,
the depths, memories of the one who got
away, the one who didn't.

Ghost Music for Shipwrecks

Embraced by the martyr's wing, wind ironed
leaves for a late-night dance, broke random bricks
against the tower of light. A mirage I'd guessed at
stuttered into view and orchestrated out again,
kept closed those closets the martyr preferred kept
open. Fans who'd hoped to see the desert sunrise
handed off their drums, mused instead on God's
shoulder, how soft it might be, how variously
it might thrum if elbowed aside—rock breaking
into skillets of yardsticks, the anarchy of throwing
dreams against glass walls, that kept all souls
solemnly epitaphed. Within the martyr's wing,
wind continued ironing leaves. Unmetered,
unmanned by untamed wind, the martyr closed
the dance, shimmered with silence, left a glance.

Hallelujah

Seventy and eighty-year-olds
teeter-totter, swing skyward,
whirl giddy on merry-go-rounds
on playgrounds.

Dare twenty-five steps to
the high diving board
they once feared to climb.

Bumper cars collide, jolt—
these oldster riders' knees
unwilling to bend, now bent
for play.

Hallelujah for dawn-gray
faces alight, fiery sun yet
to crest.

II.

Only the heart—love's cradle—
does not age:
from birth until death, it remains
the same.

—Humberto Ak'abal

Suppose

it's easy to leave yourself behind, climb
    into another's mind, say the woman sitting
across from you on the bus, her kind.

Say you leave yourself in your seat, drop into
    her memories, find a yellow-hatted monkey
dressed in blue, tail hanging by three threads,

the time her Dad belted her when she was
    just a little kid, first time she got drunk,
first marriage—she didn't love the man, not

ready to be a mom, the curly red-haired
    guy still showing up in dreams, she haunted
by mudslides, sea waiting below the cliff

to swallow her house once rains tore out
    the twisted footing. But wait. You didn't
leave yourself behind. This is her life,

the woman sitting opposite you on the bus.
    You're in it now. This middle-aged woman
stands, gathers groceries, CVS bags, walks to

the back door, exits. You stay on a few more stops,
    exit at your street, but you land on her feet,
this stranger with your gait! She's with you still,

this stranger who's no stranger, come home to share
    your life with you. Before the front hall mirror, you see
gray-white hair refusing the comb's commands, sweater

spotted with a blotch of breakfast cereal, remembering
    when your son asked for help, for money. You refused.
Now it's too late. You call nevertheless, apologize

for stinginess, or was that last year, when you should have.
    What's going on? Are you middle-aged or older, bone or
titanium-hipped? The middle-aged woman's shadow blends

with yours, a double, sort of. For a moment you doubt
    your sanity. Then you sit, relax, welcome her into your new life.

Sisyphus on Strings

I'm used to pressing piano keys,
      not plucking strings.

My fingers rebel, pained,
      pressing hard into thin steel.

I pluck the second, hope for D,
      but it sounds flat.

I loosen the peg, tighten, still don't
      get pitch right, no piano tuner to call.

I pluck a simple tune—"Turkey
      in the Straw"—half the tones sound dead.

I thought I had some music in me—
      Bach fugues, Beethoven sonatas.

I sigh, lay down the mandolin. First pebbles,
      then the whole load goes.

I pick the tyrant up, pluck the tune again,
      improved slightly—gobble if I must.

Yesterday's Takeout

In the dark magnetic morning my mirage
bangs against a beveled mirror, mountains
scatter silence into molehills that beat like
cheap aluminum pans rattling in a cupboard.
Crowbars thrust themselves at me, claiming
strength drives tongues from fruit, offer girls
repeat bright shimmerings. Crows breach the sky,
scatter caws like yardsticks measuring blue.
In the dark magnetic morning, mourning pools
its strength, pieces hours, lays them out against
the bias. Ships refuse disaster, rise whole from
wrecks, no longer indifferent to sailors' cries.
The port grows small where help abounds
or doesn't, although home recedes, spewing
ash and lava from what had been mountain.

Incidents for the Forgettery

The hundredth person on Earth diagnosed
with a rare, fatal cancer, her tissues
sent to Munich, Sao Paulo, Guangzhou,
Cape Town, to find a matching diagnosis.

She was my niece, not quite seventeen.
She died. I hated you, God. I needed her
alive. She was the person I could be if only
I had her courage—in junior high she told
the principal he should praise girls' sports,
not just brag about boys' teams.

Always engaged with life, with others,
as though it mattered. And it did. Matter.
But matter doesn't last. She died. I
screamed at you, God, as her skin faded,

blush rose to tan to dark beneath her pallor.
Till the end, she thought she'd live, saw
herself with grandkids sitting and singing
on a wide veranda. I hated you, God.
Of those I've lost, and there have been
so many, she most should have lived.

And where were you that day ropes sank
her coffin into earth? Paring your nails
beneath the apple tree? Overseeing the latest
tsunami to wash away more of Bangladesh?

Maybe Einstein was right—there's no
personal God, only a force neither malicious
nor benign, but subtly powerful, the force
behind the universe's orderly working. Did
You fail me? Did I fail myself, believing
she mattered to the world?

She died. She matters still. Do You?

Riding the Womb of the Last Wave

I paddle toward that eighty-foot wall,
arms carving long, deep strokes. I seek
the peak, pivot on the board, push with chest
and elbows, jump to stand, catch the wave's full force,
ride it to the top, knees and hips bent, weight shifted forward—
a bird, wings flying wide-open, arms rushing air,
legs riding the wave pushing me, sliding
on and on until the push is gone and I
stand on sand, turn around, paddle
toward the next last wave, ride
my mother's womb
again, again.

I saw a leatherback sea turtle

yesterday on Facebook resting on a sandy beach, dwarfing three people crouched beside it. Fact: leatherbacks can reach 1500 pounds, 7 feet in length, live 100 years or more. Will I? My pandemic hair, longer than it's been for decades, is gray. Though it's thinned, I still need clips to keep strays off eyes and lips. Yesterday the House and Senate passed the president's $1.9 trillion rescue bill. Can anyone fathom 1.9 followed by eleven zeroes' mountain of cash? How many needy people will it help? How many others will help themselves to that money? I feel overwhelmed by needs of hard-up people, pocked with remorse at what some members of my race do daily. Today on Facebook, I watched a just-hatched baby sea turtle plowing sand toward ocean with faith I hope to emulate.

Q & A Session

When from my window I watch rain fall in fall,
I ponder my life moving toward its close.
No one's fault, no one's! Some poets prefer closure,
never questioning the universe, but I like to ask
how many questions can I find answers to in this life.
Who puts limits on questions anyway! No limits
for me! But I only find answers when I stop looking
and burrow into my soul, which shines a searchlight
in the mine of who I am, a tiny person in a poor state
in a rich nation on a smallish planet sitting on the outskirts
of a largish galaxy in a universe so vast I don't even qualify
as a grain of sand. What questions would I care to pose?
None, thank you, universe. I close.

Were They Real? Where Did They Go?

Twice a year in Grampa's 1948 Chrysler,
Rob and I ride across the Cascade Mountains
from Tacoma to Yakima, to see Grampa's brother.
At the summit of the snowy pass, he stops
for gas at Texaco. We watch gas burble up,
bounce a ball in the round dome top.

While Grampa pays, Rob and I walk past
stacked motor oil cans. Beside the penny
bubble gum machine we stare again
at the tiny man and woman in a glass-front case,
each two feet tall, he in a 3-piece suit, she
in a lace-necked floor-length dress.
Seven years old, I read:

>   *This man and woman were missionaries*
>   *to a Peruvian tribe that captured, shrank them.*
>   *Each had been a full-sized adult.*

Rob and I don't know death. We're astonished
people can be shrunk, their bodies stay proportional
in size and shape. Their sewn-shut eyes, her hand
missing a tiny fingernail, magnetize our eyes.

That gas station closed half a century ago.
Where did the couple go? Were they real?
I don't know what to hope.

Texas Hold'em

Middle-aged, both dealt hands
of busted marriages, who'd have guessed
by betting on our messy lives, we'd thrive?
I'd forgotten how to trust, folded men
quicker than I'd hold 'em. You'd lost
the chair, one chip left. Antes high,
hard to make the call. And yet...
three decades later, we still spoon
to warm each other's flesh, cook
together, feast on shared ideas.
A once in a lifetime hand,
that royal flush.

Make It Red

This slumped glass glazed red slopes in
on all four sides, catches light like eyes,
like a mind. Smoothly cool, a child's
glowing face come inside from snow.

No hint of orange or a child's fire-engine,
this red's been tempered by some grief,
some death. Dark as Revlon's *Ravish Me Red*—
love's touch, once burning hot, then lost.

Not found on rainbow's spectrum,
this red's made by fusing darker glass
to lighter, to deepen, heighten, become
the color of my blood as it departs

oxygen-rich lungs, the color of my life
moving, moving on, a glorious red, the artist
made for me to marvel at, this blown glass
that will pass into unknown hands.

Death Grabs the Pommel

Death's minions fell on him . . . .
The first stole muscles one by one . . . .
Another carried off a gland . . . .
The third looted flesh, got away . . . .
The fourth shoplifted breath . . . .
The last pilfered his brain, couldn't . . . .
New light seeps into the room . . . .
Where he no longer lies, bed empty . . . .
Hoyer lift hangs useless after the fact . . . .
 Behind a barred door . . . .
 Through an open window . . . .
 We don't know and so
 We wait in limbo
 Want him back
 Want him well
 Grateful he was here

Mounts, Rides Off

He tried to fight them off . . . .
They just kept coming . . . .
It wasn't fair—he didn't stand a chance . . . .
I know—good people and bad things, but . . . .
We lose hope . . . .
Earth's indifferent to pain . . . .
Sunrise, dawn—a mockery . . . .
Then a moonless night's deeper truth . . . .
He's gone . . .where?

Still

Litter curries the highway shoulder,
curries but cannot comb it as trucks
fly by, make fly-ups fly away,
before rain soaks the sodden mass
of plastic bags, cigarette butts,
fast-food cups and all lies still.

The razor in her hand stills
an arcing sweep, tender wrist
she could cut, but won't tonight.

An erhu's sound haunts me, its
python-skin overtones vibrating
in what I still call my soul,
though I don't know what
it means to say *my soul.*

Arthritic fingers still long to touch
my piano's keys, distill the music
they remember, until I recall my eyes
cannot fill themselves with notes
upon the page, cannot build
the sound that thrilled my soul.

Ode to This Body Coming Up
on Eighty-Four Years

You lifer, what a sentence you were handed!
Yet you kept surviving. Migraines stomped

your head until hot flashes stopped, age seventy-nine.
Rheumatic fever slugged your heart three times.

Lungs tried swamp crawls, decided they like
dry air. Stomach holds you hostage to fat-free

cottage cheese, forbids favorites—single-malt
scotch, chocolate, coffee. Giant colon hoards

poop like Fort Knox gold. Eyesight knifed for piano.
Kidneys going, hearing too, but ok with aids.

Titanium right hip, steroids to knee and hand,
many times under knife for carpal tunnel.

Once you almost said goodbye, but triple antibiotics
brought you back from bird flu and pneumonia.

Young, I beat you up as useless, always getting sick,
trusted brain for Latin, lit & trig. Old, I'm grateful

we're still together. I'll keep singing like a canary
in a cage till I hear you say, *Let's blow this aviary.*

Cache

They gleam, those deep blue bottles
in my friend's sunny kitchen window.
She points to her big back yard, *Want
some?* I see an open pit two feet deep.

Before garbage trucks, she explains,
says the previous owners lived here
seventy years till they sold in the 1950s.
I kneel, see a cache of blue bottles.

Dirt fills their mouths, settles inside,
obscures the faded label. I brush off
Maine's granite soil, scrape till faded
colors appear, words missing a few letters.

I read *Dr. Thom son's Sp cial Lad es
Formul . For Th se Month y Blu s.
32% alcoho , a dash of code ne.*
Dozens of bottles, dozens.

The Ladies' Friend.

chaos descended

fell on me like 20 squabbling banty roosters

not one to enter a losing fray
              I backed off
saw frog spawn floating on the pond
                    obscured koi I'd come to watch
reversed steps
          backtracked to the boulder
where I transform confusion into clarity
                 found lichen covering its top
                     clarity concealed

then sun failed to shine

    then rain failed to fall

        then wind blew unceasing

I took out worry beads
dark stones
smoothed from use
fingered their surfaces

found roosters squabbling
             frog spawn floating
                     lichen obscuring

said to myself

I'll grab the loose end of chaos

twine it about this dream of thriving I used to have

see whether chaos wants a little re-direction

III.

Trampoline of green-green moss under our shoes! Hello!
We're inside our lives. The wood is wide. And close around us.

——Nomi Stone

Grief Speaks

Earth says: *Why have you buried these little bodies
in me? They should be running, leaping,
shouting, not silent in their coffins. Who
didn't watch over them? Protect them
when they couldn't do it for themselves?*

Sun says: *Not me. I shone to help them play
outside, grow strong bones.*

Rain says: *Not me. I splattered puddles so when
they jumped they'd splash, have fun.*

Teachers say: *Not us. We died with them, tried
to keep them living till the shooter said
good night, and took our lives.*

Moms say: *Not me. I loved my child before I birthed her.
That morning I kissed her good-bye as she left
for school, how can it be the last?*

Dads say: *Not me. I taught him how to throw a ball,
swing a bat, to find magic in stories. How
can that last hug carry me through life?*

Shooters say: *Bullies called me loser when I was little,
never stopped. So I stopped lives of little kids.
Then cops stopped mine.*

Cops say: *We were terrified—we've got families too.
He had an AR-15, we had Glocks. He could
have mowed us down before we stopped him.*

Gun salesman says: *The look on that kid's face*
         worried me. What could I do? He had
         a legal right to buy, he was eighteen.

Senators say: *Re-election's coming up. I face*
         a tough opponent who'd slaughter me
         if I supported gun control.

Earth says: *Who's left to keep kids safe?*

Wind says: *Whooooooooooooooooooooyouuuuuuu*

Learning to Hum

I've been a long time sculpting me,
shaping each part into curves I admire,
finding the best degree from head to heart.
Just as I'm getting it right, I'll need to leave
myself to go with death. Leaf detaching
from the tree, I'll nourish what comes next.

It's a shame, the suffering into learning into
a sort of wisdom I can't infuse in anyone.
We make our path, often muddy, flesh
scarred by error, unmoored, abandoned by
our own best self. We cast a line, anchor it
in hope, reel in what we can, sometimes
a broken shoe, a fish too big to land.

Sometimes the border's closed, the fence
too high to climb, the porridge too hot
or a love gone cold. Not the bed we wanted,
but we climb in, hum the tune our mothers
hummed to us, radiate the small that's
all we are.

At Five I Learn Delight

Gramp lets me crank the handle.
When it's too stiff he takes over,
rock salt riding on the ice block
he splintered with a sledgehammer
to pack around the tub. When he
can barely turn the crank, he
pronounces it done, and Gram
brings spoons and bowls, scoops
mounds of ice cream thick with
peaches she picked that morning.
We perch like birds on their back steps
spooning sweetness, of peaches
and cream, replete with one
achievement made by three.

Ode to My Hearing Aids on Valentine's Day

Snips of snails and puppy dog tails
I tuck at morning into each ear
and at night place in their charger,
you connect, making me present
and a presence in an otherwise
receding world.

Microchip receiver, minute mic,
you magnify sounds I miss,
especially initial ones—did I hear
save or *fave, fare* or *there?*

Without you I can't tell; with you,
I make a better guess. Yet, for years
I resisted you, didn't want to know
my lack. Smiling, serene, silent, I
missed the more vivid living.

As when cataracts grayed my world,
my ears turned music gray as I lost
crescendos, diminuendos. Did I hear
a clarinet or violin?

Finally I gave in, hoped no one would
notice your snails curled inside my ears
like pets, everywhere except in bed.
For returning me to the world's terror,
its beauty, its love, I thank you.

Hope Is a Gizzard,

thick walls enclosing grit, preparing us
for pain, helps us grind, digest, integrate,
go on. But the child whom cancer takes?
Woman whom marriage fails, poverty
succeeds? Man who fights for country,
returns one leg less? Such loss sticks in
the gizzard while hope waves in the
distance, a yellow rose, bud opening,
whose aroma tickles the nose.

The Asteroid

Dinosaurs didn't get that they were doomed
the day that asteroid climbed the sky, then
smashed the Yucatan Peninsula, incinerating
much of life on Earth. Choking dust, tsunamis,
years of no sunlight did the rest. It took a while
but mammals benefited from the raid, leading
to a human population boom: deserts growing,
glaciers nearly gone, oceans too acidic for their
creatures, summers hotter, winters shorter, warmer.
We extract and trash, despite our inklings of extinction.
We won't need an asteroid. We are the asteroid.

Out of Hopeful Green Stuff

Drab brown trees bely the still green grass.
Their nudity contrasts earth's keen cover, grass.

I find a four-leaf clover hiding in the back yard.
No extra luck, but my bare toes like the feel of grass.

Childhood chore: root out clover growing in lawn.
I fill paper bags with it, find treasures in grass.

Whitman's response, *The handkerchief of the Lord*,
when in his poem a child asks, *What is the grass?*

Roots, stem, leaf, flower—unite to make the whole.
Together, multitudes gleam in an acre of grass.

A democratic field: all plants receive enough
when sun and rain team up to feed the grass.

Hairstory

At three, Mom cascades
gold curls down my back
that ripple in the wind as
I push my toy mower in
tall grass, laugh when green
blades bend and stand back up
like Mom in the aftermath
of Dad's bouts. I'm cast iron,
dense throughout, grief-weighted.

My first beauty shop visit
at fifteen, Mr. George cuts,
styles, sprays my hair into
a helmet I can't remove.
In the mirror a stranger
stares back at me. I don't
know who I want to be.

Pregnant at twenty-three,
my love and I sample coffee
in Manhattan's all-night cafes,
walk the dark away. Love wings us,
but in two years he'll fly, abandon
our child and me. I've barely met
myself.

By thirty-five I surprise myself,
good at motherhood. My hair fares
poorly when the auburn wig I wear
to have the color I want singes,
removing a turkey from the oven,

rather like my fantasy of a man
who won't try to force my circle
into his square.

At fifty, I move to teach in Appalachia.
My gray hair swings at wild turkey
calling contests, dances to Scots-Irish music.
I meet a man who matches my geometry,
in love for keeps. As each year passes,
I toss old anguish out, invite in delight.

At eighty-three, my child sixty,
grandchildren young adults,
I twist sparse hair in a gray-
white bun. Wisps straggle,
unwilling to be fixed, grown
butterfly light. I'm emergent,
wings still wet—at the right time
I'll fly away. Not yet.

Unraveling

Cicadas' red eyes disappear, reappear
on schedule, their lives not unraveling
as ours do through excess that sometimes
does us in. We handle certain rhythms
well—ribcage expanding with each breath;
so too, the arching backbone when in sex
each vertebra adjusts with thrusts.

Other rhythms not so well—the daily drink
topped off with six, anger that doesn't give,
until it finds a nearby target. Cicadas get
five molts before they reach adulthood.
Molting might have saved some teenage kids
who'd still be breathing if heroin hadn't
undone them, if Suboxone, recovery centers,
hadn't failed them—if society hadn't shed them
like exoskeletons.

We survive the stages of our lives until
we don't. Who knew we shared body parts
with cicadas: heart, anus, femur, tibia.
Perhaps we should practice some form
of shedding—clear our minds and hearts
with whatever meditation works, molt
the old thinking and emotions, fly on
new-grown wings.

My First, My Last

I'd never caved, but in southwestern Washington a cave
beckoned. Up for trying something new, I signed on:
cave known, no dangers, good for beginners.

The leader wore a headlamp, entered easy on hands
and knees. Near the end of a dozen cavers, I crawled in.
When his headlight disappeared, entrance light lingered.

Suddenly no light left, the darkest dark, blackest black,
worse than childhood fears of bogeymen creeping
attic stairs to my bedroom. No glow, no seep of light.

Back rubbing now, I flattened onto belly, hands ahead.
Grabbing dust, I pulled my body as walls pressed against
my back and sides, barely room to breathe.

Two cavers behind me, only one way out, through
a birth canal crowded with siblings, my throat
burned with screams I ate raw not to erupt.

Eons passed before dim light showed. I emerged,
with a soft cry, reborn a claustrophobic.

Tossing the Dice of Language

Word, unmoored word—what language
cannot hold onto, some ledge of words
to rest on, a subtle match, a breath
from the wind god.

The sound waves of train tracks mimic
coming night. Outside, air thickens
with cold. The dark of an empty house
trolls the uncertainties of ground,
empty the next morning.

Cast back the light, the possibility
of beauty traced out with both hands
lined by life and passion. There's always
a border straight and naked, precise as a map,
like a river inside a slipper, a zipper whip
of color, three parts rage trying to look dire.
All of it was trouble.

Trouble, all of it.
Dire, trying to look like rage, three parts color
whipped and zipped inside a slipper, river
like a map, precise and naked, straight border
always there. Passion and life-lined,
both hands traced out with beauty,
possibility to light back, cast
morning next to empty, ground
uncertain, trolling the house
empty of dark, cold with thick air.
Outside, night coming, mimicking
tracks, train of waves, sounding

God from the wind, breath a match,
subtle, a rest of words, ledge
onto some hold, cannot language
word, what, unmoored, the Word?

IV.

I can't
explain it, but my life is rising into the air.
It's lifting me. My life is rising and taking me with it.

—Maggie Smith

Your Name Is a Wound Is a Song

I saved your last message in my email, Sharon,
the one about Laurie Anderson, whose art and
voice we both admire. What sweetness lingers

in your wake—for me, sudden, unexpected.
When I said I'd phone again next month, I thought
we'd have more time. Christmas came, New Year's—

and then my daughter's call—*She's gone, three
nights ago.* I've spoken with you ever since.
You tell me death arrived just right—grabbed

you after pain mounted its high horse, held you
to the saddle, galloped where I can't follow.
You're okay with death—you did the myriad things

you meant to do, inspired 4,000 students to reach
beyond easy—to volunteer at food banks,
stage mock debates at election time—gave them

tastes of Shakespeare plays in Oregon. You made
your money work for justice, marched in protests,
lived the better part of nine decades mostly happy,

steamed around Drake Passage, Cape Horn,
awed by night's billion stars, impoverished Cuba's
murals, dancing, music night and day. But I'm here

and you're not—emptiness where we had fullness.
This summer I'll be in Washington State.
You won't. April's forsythias didn't burst as bright

this spring. Red tulips barely moved past orange.
On the bush below my window, frost-damaged leaves.
We outlive ourselves, dear Sharon. We go on.

Sometimes I Disappear

Deep clefts, islands long grown
apart. Fissures draw till all resides
inside, nothing left of the person
I call me.

Black rifts sycamore's skin, blotched
like old age spots, peeling white reveals
gray on its way to white. I'm there,

gray turning white, separating
into black, falling to earth,
nothing left of me.

On a visit, I lift through desert sky,
lingering sunset lighting saguaros,
above western moon, stars between
black rifts, holding light.

Home again, over eastern night,
I descend to my desk, seeing clearly
with weakening eyes as I continue
disappearing into earth, holding light.

Spring

Fresh-caught
from an April pond,
the two-inch salamander
wriggles frantic
in a plastic pail,
when the six-year-old
touches finger to its skin.
She tells her little sister
Let's wriggle together.
Their lithe bodies squirm,
zigzag as they slither,
then squat, rise on toothpick
legs, giggle. *Again! Let's
do it again!* Three beings
moving together as one,
in fear, and joy.

To Be or Not To Be

When the old timers at Rock Lake
used to say in late fall, *The woolly bears
are everywhere, that means a hard winter,*
I couldn't step without accidentally
squishing the bristly black and orange
banded caterpillars. *The more black,
the more snow and ice*, and they were right.
That January I saw on the frozen lake
ten cars, five bikers doing wheelies,
figure eights, where other winters, none
ventured to test their weight on thin ice.

Spring came late. Out walking our dog,
I heard lake ice crack, groan and grind,
jamming ice blocks against the dam.
Large chunks toppled and crashed,
but woollies held safe haven in cocoons
on shrubs or ground blanketed by last fall's
leaves, occupied with the weather
of metamorphosis, to be or not to be
tiger moths, and fly.

Hidden Valley Liturgy

If not for the river, the road (drivable)
If not for the road, the cabin (built sixty years)
If not for the cabin (gathering three generations)
If not for the gathering (caught by hot fir)
      no need to let the dead alone (who keep rising)
Let alone their intention (still warm toward the living)
Till dead, the living keep rising, falling (like rising,
      drifting smoke)
Drift filling the valley (hiding the hills)
Fires burning firs on the mountain (orange eating green)
The mountain worshiping (new snow)
The worship of firs soughing in wind (singing birds
      to rest)
At rest, the gathering in the cabin (at rest on the road)
No rest for the smoke (or the flames racing near)
Flames racing nearer, intent on the living
      (intent on the dead)

Heart

I peer inside, find my heart, organ
known to spill over, topple heavy,
broken hay bale scattered on I-5.
I scour my history of love—wounds,
wonders, trading scorched miles
for gold-paved roads, some noosed
as I gasped, flashed on when I first said

I love you to you, memory scattered
among decades' blossoms. When I
slip into the land of *no return*, don't
chase after me. Keep your roots intact,
rooted in love. Hold on, grow more
seasons in the light of those who love you.
If you're first to go, I'll need to learn

to root in granite, cracking open rock
to survive in clefts. Yet, with what else
shall we gift our children, than with
courage to endure? If we have another
life, let's find each other at our special
place. You'll know me by my wind-swept
eagle wings, my fiercely tender heart.

Hope Is a Grasshopper

Watch it leap. Last night I tweezed out a curly stand-up eyebrow hair. Inter-groper. Doctor said *macular degeneration both eyes, dry type, retinal detachments. Nothing I can do.* Sorry. Grace-hoper. Last year I played my last Bach, piano a corpse in the corner of my study. Grail-loper. I see dust moats on my computer screen, desk lamp. Can't see notes on a music staff. Are those 8th notes, 16^{ths} or a bird in flight? Is that a C or E two octaves above middle C, or the bird returning, bug in beak? Hop. Grief-holder. Hop.

Silent before Eternity

Before eternity, your stomachs sat atop your digging feet,
hence your name, Gastropoda, a Mollusk. Your family
went extinct 300 million years ago though snails
and slugs continue to thrive. As seas receded,
your feet vanished as ancient sand trapped
them, your whorls of cream and darkish
gleam—fossil I bought on eBay, three
of you in the rock someone hacked
from sandstone cliffs, polished to
glitter in my study before life
completed a Fibonacci
whorl of descending
size. I stand silent
before your
eternal
now.

My Life with Rivers

I come from rivers, though I live on land.
Began where the Mississippi rises
from Minnesota ground, loped west
with the Missouri, till it turned south
and I strayed north. Followed the Blackwater
far as I could, caught the Snake and side-winded
as rivers wended me west till Columbia carried me
to Puget Sound, where waves carved chunks from hills.
I fled inland, where I heard rivers calling me east
to Michigan, to Chicago where I paused on the lake,
kept flowing until I finally landed, at home
on the Monongahela. Where now shall I roam,
what rivers beyond the River Styx, flowing
to who knows what end?

The Suitor

Let down your hair
That I may climb thy golden stair
            —The Brothers Grimm

He arrives, driving
a top-down red Corvette—

        Not frightening as I expected,
        attractive, really, wavy hair,
        Ray Bans, smoking a pipe—
                do I let him climb?

I could toss my gray braid
from the upstairs window to him,
my latest love, my last

            having already packed my go-bag
            of bacon rind, jerky, and pemmican.

He walks from the car, carrying
something in floral tissue

        I'd like to stay in my small condo,
        admire the Navajo pots I bought,
        see orchids send up stems, ripen buds,
        bloom their lovely purples,

        give my piano Mozart one last time,
        hear Beethoven's late quartets again
        whose silent moments glisten toward eternity.

He strides loose-hipped, long-legged,

carries wolfsbane and white lilies—

      At my window I wait—

      do I greet him smiling . . .

      say *I'm not quite ready* . . .

      request he *try again next year* . . .

Twenty Existential Questions

In the center of her web a spider waits.
>   What do you await?

Below her web, soil might be a century old
>   or newly churned from an earthworm's gut.

Have your guts churned lately?
>   How long do you plan to live?

When you last kissed your love, did you live?
>   Did the earth quake? Did you?

I quake when I consider blocks—
>   city blocks, Lego blocks, writer's block.

Plaything, will you unblock me? Let's play stars.
>   Shall we make gold stars worth more than silver?

A row of stars for good comportment:
>   Four stars for those who lost a name, who died.

My name, changeless as a politician's taste for scandal.
>   Which school for scandal did you choose?

Was it fun? Inspiring? Did you graduate?
>   What good is your degree if you hide it?

We'll not hide today's specials. Will you have
>   cod on rye with mayo and mustard?

Tomorrow comes with ketchup, no substitutes.
>   Do you come? Come when called?

I call a spade a spade. What do you call clubs?
      I dislike weapons, but enjoy dance clubs in disco dress.

Are your windows dressed? Do you wear undies under slacks?
      I'm slacking off—back to log booms:

When the boom breaks, to what sea will the logs migrate?
      When you break, will you find a warm sea to empty into?

Time,

you slick, you slippery beast. Of prey and
play. Full of yourself, aren't you, Time?

Full and empty. Took six million years
to get us here. Now we're at the abyss, Time:

unseasonal seasons, wars ramped up, healing
hiding out. But hey, that's us, not you, Time.

The baby asleep, thumb in mouth, her sister watching
the Slinky skip down stairs better than she can walk, Time,

what time have they? For Einstein, you're space's fourth
dimension, yet he thought you illusion, reality timeless. Time,

wish I could agree, but thinning hair, wrinkled skin,
slowed brain declare I'm in a losing race, Time.

Rushing to buy groceries, to the bank for cash, prepare
a meal we'll want to eat—never enough time, Time-

as-Chronos. But time-as-Kairos—arrow's perfect shot,
coloratura hits high G, penis and clitoris sing, Time!

The moment doesn't last, though we get the high.
This counts, that brief stay against you, Time.

What's new lures me—latest ChatGPT, Webb Telescope's
wanderings, soapstone for storing sun's heat, Time.

And tide ebbs faster than it floods. Quite a ride it's been,
bumpy, beauteous—but I'm running out on you, Time.

Notes

[11] Epigraph comes from Ed Skoog, "Tomato Poem."

[25] Epigraph comes Humberto Ak'abal, "The Color of Mist."

[26] Title comes from CM Burroughs's poem of the same title in *Master Suffering*.

[43] Phrase "loose end of chaos" comes from He Xiang's "Two Rolls," *The American Poetry Review*, September / October 2020.

[45] Epigraph comes from Nomi Stone, "This Island Is Called Mull."

[58] The first half of "Tossing the Dice of Language" is a cento, the sources of which come from poems of Grace Bauer, Jeanmarie Evelly, Michele Graaff, Danusha Laméris, Stephen Morrow, Tyler Mortensen-Hayes, Anna Newman, James Ragan, Denzel Scott, Kathleen Balma, Susan Browne, Barbara Lydecker, Maya Tevet Dayan, Daniel Arias Gomez, Kimberly Kemler, James Davis May, Gabrielle Otero, Bruce Beasley, Rajiv Mohabir, Cynthia Arrieu-King, and Kazim Ali.

[61] Epigraph comes from Maggie Smith, "On the Occasion of My Feet Inexplicably Leaving the Ground."

[67] Kasey Jueds's "Litany (Paulownia)" is the model for "Hidden Valley Liturgy."

photo: Tom Miles

SUSAN SHAW SAILER has previously published three books of poems— *The Distance Beyond Sight*, *The God of Roundabouts*, *Ship of Light*—and two chapbooks, *Bulletins from a War Zone* and *COAL*. Sailer lives in Morgantown, West Virginia, and is a member of the Madwomen in the Attic program of Carlow University and also of Pauletta Hansel's From Draft to Craft class. She was a professor of English at West Virginia University and before that taught English in Tacoma Public Schools.

www.ingramcontent.com/pod-product-compliance
Lightning Source LLC
Chambersburg PA
CBHW022038090426
42741CB00007B/1115